CREATURES OF LEGEND

UNICORNS

by Megan Atwood

Content Consultant
Joseph Nigg
Author of *Wonder Beasts*
and other books on mythical animals

CORE
LIBRARY

Published by ABDO Publishing Company, PO Box 398166, Minneapolis, MN 55439. Copyright © 2014 by Abdo Consulting Group, Inc. International copyrights reserved in all countries. No part of this book may be reproduced in any form without written permission from the publisher. The Core Library™ is a trademark and logo of ABDO Publishing Company.

Printed in the United States of America,
North Mankato, Minnesota
102013
012014

THIS BOOK CONTAINS AT LEAST 10% RECYCLED MATERIALS.

Editor: Lauren Coss
Series Designer: Becky Daum

Library of Congress Cataloging-in-Publication Data
Atwood, Megan.
 Unicorns / by Megan Atwood.
    pages cm. -- (Creatures of legend)
 Includes index.
 ISBN 978-1-62403-153-3
 1. Unicorns--Juvenile literature. I. Title.
 GR830.U6A88 2014
 398.24'54--dc23
                                    2013027278

Photo Credits: Shutterstock Images, cover, 1; Thinkstock, 4, 7, 8, 20, 29, 30, 34, 41 (top left), 41 (top right), 42, 43 (bottom), 45; Flip Nicklin/Minden Pictures/Corbis, 10; Alexandra Day/Corbis, 12; Photos.com/Thinkstock, 14; Jane Sweeney/JAI/Corbis, 18; David Whinham/Demotix/Corbis, 23; Corbis, 26; David Robertson/Alamy, 32; Robinet Testard/National Library, St. Petersburg, Russia/The Bridgeman Art Library, 33; Center of Natural Sciences/AP Images, 36; Jensen Farley Pictures/Everett Collection, 39; Red Line Editorial, 41 (main), 43 (top)

CONTENTS

CHAPTER ONE

A LEGEND OF THE UNICORN

The king of Friesland loved his daughter, Isabel, very much. One day he gave her a unicorn as a gift. The unicorn was pure white. It had a long, flowing mane. A single horn twisted out of its forehead. It was a beautiful creature.

Isabel loved her unicorn. She rode it all over the kingdom. Soon people in the kingdom began calling her the Lady of the Unicorn. A young man named

Unicorn legends can be found in cultures around the world. Some tales date back thousands of years.

The Lion and the Unicorn

In the Middle Ages, symbols were used to identify different European groups. These symbols appeared on shields known as coats of arms. A coat of arms could represent a family, an army, or even an entire nation. In the 1500s, England and Scotland were ruled separately. England's coat of arms had two lions. Scotland's coat of arms had two unicorns. In 1603 King James VI of Scotland inherited the English throne. He changed his name to King James I. He combined the two countries' coats of arms. This represented the unification of England and Scotland.

Bartholomew was in love with Isabel. Bartholomew was no ordinary young man. He rode a lion. He was known as the Knight of the Lion. Isabel soon fell in love with him too.

Kidnapped!

One day a messenger came to Isabel and lied to her. He told her Bartholomew was dead. Isabel was heartbroken. Then the messenger kidnapped her and took her to a castle far away. A dragon guarded the castle.

The Knight of the Lion soon learned Isabel

A stone unicorn stands guard outside a Scottish castle.

had been captured. He knew he had to save her.
Bartholomew rode to the castle on his lion. When
he got there, the dragon looked big and scary.

In most Western legends, the unicorn resembles a white horse with a single horn coming out of its forehead.

Bartholomew wasn't sure how he would save Isabel. But he made up his mind to attack the dragon.

Bartholomew drew his sword. Riding his lion, he attacked the dragon. The dragon blew fire and smoke at him. Bartholomew had to retreat. He tried to get closer to stab the dragon with his sword. But every time he got within striking distance, the heat from the dragon drove him back. How could he possibly get close to the dragon without burning himself and his lion alive?

The Unicorn Saves the Day

Just as Bartholomew was about to give up, he heard hooves beating on the ground. Looking back, he saw Isabel's unicorn coming up the path toward the dragon. The unicorn ran at the dragon, its horn lowered to strike. As the unicorn got closer, the dragon blew fire and smoke at the creature. But nothing happened. The fire bounced off the unicorn's skin. The unicorn plunged its horn into the dragon, killing it.

Real-Life Unicorns

Few people believe in unicorns today. But a narwhal could be a close cousin of the mythical creature. A narwhal is a sea mammal, similar to a dolphin, porpoise, or whale. Narwhals live in the Arctic Ocean. Each narwhal has a large tooth that spirals out of its upper lip. The tooth looks a lot like a horn coming out of its forehead. This tooth can grow to be up to eight feet (2.4 m) long. For hundreds of years, people mistook narwhal teeth for unicorn horns.

At one time, many people thought narwhal teeth were unicorn horns.

Isabel ran from the castle and threw her arms around the unicorn. Then the Knight of the Lion and the Lady of the Unicorn climbed onto their animals. They rode away together.

A Horned Horse

The story of Isabel and Bartholomew is just one of the many folktales involving the unicorn. This European tale is from the Middle Ages. The Middle Ages lasted from approximately the 400s to the 1400s CE. Although the story is hundreds of years old, the unicorn it describes is similar to unicorns we know today.

EXPLORE ONLINE

In the past, some people believed narwhal teeth were unicorn horns. The Web site at the link below discusses narwhals. As you know, every source is different. How is the information on the Web site different from the information on narwhals in this chapter? How is it the same? After reading about narwhals on the Web site, can you think of any other characteristics that may have caused people to confuse narwhals with unicorns?

Narwhals
www.mycorelibrary.com/unicorns

CHAPTER TWO

UNICORN CHARACTERISTICS

Today most people know unicorns are not real. But the idea of the unicorn has captured imaginations for centuries. According to most modern legends, a unicorn is a big, white, magical horse with a long, twisting horn coming out of its forehead. The unicorn is said to live forever unless it is killed. It is known for being gentle. Some unicorns

In many legends, unicorns are said to live in forests.

In some myths, unicorns have goat-like beards.

even have wings. In nearly all legends, unicorns have magical powers.

The magical white unicorn of today got its look almost 2,000 years ago. It was described in a book called the *Physiologus*. An unknown author put the book together in the 100s CE. The *Physiologus* is known as a bestiary. A bestiary is a book about types of animals. Some of the animals in the *Physiologus* are real, and some are mythical.

The *Physiologus* describes the unicorn as a strong animal. It is very sly and careful. The only way to capture the creature is for a young woman to lure it to hunters. The *Physiologus* unicorn is more like a goat than a horse. But it still has a horn. According to some versions of the *Physiologus*, this horn can purify water just by touching it. The *Physiologus* spread the idea of unicorns, and their popularity increased throughout Christian Europe in the Middle Ages.

Creating a Unicorn

In the 1930s, Dr. W. Franklin Dove created a unicorn from a bull. He wanted to prove that a bull's horn tissue was different than skull tissue. When the bull calf was one day old, Dove performed surgery on it so it would have one horn instead of two. Dove removed the horn buds and put them in the center of the bull's forehead. When put together, the two horn buds grew into one horn. Dove's bull became the leader of its herd. The bull used its horn to plow under fences. It also used the horn to defend itself. Having one horn helped the bull!

Magical Powers

The most magical part of the unicorn is said to be its horn. The horn can guard against poison. It also heals diseases. In the Middle Ages, some people ground up rhinoceros horns and walrus tusks. Then they sold the powder as unicorn horn. Many people bought these powders to protect themselves from poisons.

The small, goat-like creature of the *Physiologus* was the main source of unicorn legends in the West.

It would eventually evolve into the magical, white unicorn we often think of today. However, in the East, the unicorn was a very different kind of animal than the one described in the *Physiologus*.

CHAPTER THREE

EASTERN UNICORNS

The Asian unicorn may have been written about as long ago as 2700 BCE. It became a very important part of the folklore of many Eastern countries.

The Qilin

In China the unicorn is known as the *qilin*. The qilin looks similar to a calf. But it has shiny scales like a dragon. It also has one horn growing out of its head.

The Asian qilin was shown in many different ways. In this temple painting, its horn looks like an elephant trunk.

Qilins have been an important part of Chinese mythology for thousands of years.

One ancient qilin myth says the first man was named Pan Gu. Using a mallet, Pan Gu sculpted the world into existence, creating the universe. A dragon, a tortoise, a *fenghuang* (the Chinese version of a phoenix), and a qilin helped Pan Gu. According to the legend, each of these animals was in charge of one part of the earth. The qilin was in charge of the forests.

The qilin was said to appear in a forest as a sign of good luck when an emperor was kind and just. A qilin's appearance was also said to predict the birth or death of a great leader.

Confucius and the Unicorn

Confucius was a Chinese teacher and philosopher who lived from 551 to 479 BCE. Many of his teachings are still used today. According to some versions of the legend, a qilin visited Confucius's mother, Ching-tsae, when she was pregnant with him. The creature nuzzled up to Ching-tsae. When she opened her hand, she saw that the qilin had given her a piece of jade. Words

One Chinese legend credits unicorns for inventing Chinese writing more than 5,000 years ago. According to the legend, a qilin walked up to Chinese emperor Fu Xi and stomped its leg three times. The emperor noticed that the qilin had signs and symbols all over its body. Fu Xi stared at them as the qilin turned to walk away. He quickly found a stick and began writing the lines and symbols down in the dirt beside him. These symbols became the first written language of China.

were written on the jade, giving a prophecy. The words said Ching-tsae's son would be a great man—a "throneless king." Ching-tsae tied a white ribbon around the qilin's horn.

Toward the end of Confucius's life, he learned that the qilin who visited his mother had been captured. Confucius went to see the creature. He saw the same ribbon tied around its horn.

Confucius knew then that his time in the world was at an end. He died peacefully.

The qilin was reportedly seen only once after Confucius, by an emperor named Wudi. Then it

Traditional Vietnamese unicorn dances are still performed today in many parts of the world.

disappeared for years. But the legend continued. In 1415 Chinese emperor Zhu Di sent some of his people on an expedition to Africa. The sailors came back with a gift for him. They called it a unicorn.

But the emperor knew right away it wasn't a unicorn. The sailors had given him a giraffe!

The Kirin

Japan has its own unicorn lore as well. The Japanese version of the unicorn is known as a *kirin*. The kirin has a dragon's head, a deer's body, a horse's legs, and a dragon's scales. It is often shown with either antlers or the single horn widely known today in unicorn lore.

According to Japanese myths, some rulers used kirins in court cases. The kirin helped decide who was innocent and who was guilty. Legend says the kirin always knew who was guilty. It immediately speared the criminal in the chest.

During Zhu Di's reign, a unicorn song was sung in Annam, China, which is now Vietnam. During the song, archers shot at a representation of a unicorn. It was believed that when this song ended, monsoon rains would begin:

The unicorn's hoofs!

The duke's sons throng.

Alas for the unicorn!

The unicorn's brow!

The duke's kinsmen throng.

Alas for the unicorn!

The unicorn's horn!

The duke's clansmen throng.

Alas for the unicorn!

Source: Nancy Hathaway. The Unicorn. New York: Viking Press, 1984. Print. 51.

Consider Your Audience

What do you think is happening in this song? If you had to write this out as a story, how would you tell it? Write a story for young children conveying the information presented in the song.

CHAPTER FOUR

WESTERN UNICORNS

The first Western written account of a unicorn came from the Greek physician Ctesias in the late 400s BCE. The account appeared in a book about India. Ctesias actually didn't see the unicorn himself. He heard its description from people he encountered who had traveled to India.

A Western unicorn is shown in a Dutch tapestry titled "The Unicorn in Captivity," which was created in the 1500s.

Many Colors

Many people think Ctesias's source was actually describing a species of wild donkey that lives in India. This real animal has a reddish body and a white underbelly. Some think that Ctesias's storytellers were putting two animals together—the wild donkey and the rhinoceros. Some wonder if the horn colors Ctesias describes could have come from a horn that had been decorated with paint.

Rhino or Unicorn?

Ctesias's creature looks like a wild donkey. Its feet are similar to an elephant's. Unlike the white unicorn of today, the creature Ctesias describes is many different colors. It has a white body, a dark red head, and dark blue eyes. It has a horn that is white at the bottom, black in the middle, and red at the tip. This horn was said to have healing properties. According to Ctesias, drinking out of a unicorn horn was said to stop epilepsy and to make the drinker immune to poison.

Could Ctesias's witnesses have been describing a wild Indian donkey?

Many people have guessed what animal Ctesias's source really saw. Some believe Ctesias is actually describing a rhinoceros. Many people still believe rhinoceros horns have healing abilities. However, Ctesias's description doesn't exactly fit the rhinoceros. A rhinoceros has a horn on its nose rather than its head. A rhino is also much bigger than a wild donkey.

Some historians believe both Pliny the Elder and Gaius Julius Solinus were describing rhinoceroses.

One possibility is that people returning to Greece were actually describing a combination of two animals.

More Ancient Unicorns

In approximately the 70s CE, Roman scholar Pliny the Elder described another kind of unicorn. His creature had a stag's head, elephant feet, and a boar's tail. The creature also had a single black horn in the middle of its forehead. Pliny's unicorn was said to be fierce and impossible to capture.

In the 200s CE, another Roman, Gaius Julius Solinus, wrote a book called *Polyhistor*, which included a description of unicorns. Solinus's unicorn was based on Pliny the Elder's description. But Solinus added that the creature had a horrible bellow, or call. Today many people think Solinus was describing a rhinoceros.

In later years, the unicorn gained popularity because of the Christian Bible. In the early 400s CE Saint Jerome translated the Bible from Greek into Latin. The Greek word *monokeros* was translated to Latin's *unicornis*. Both words mean "one horn." More than 1,000 years later, in 1611, the King James English version of the bible used the word *unicorn*. The word became

The Name of a Unicorn

How did the unicorn first get into the Bible? Some historians believe this first happened when scholars translated the Old Testament of the Bible from Hebrew into Greek in the 200s BCE. The translators knew the Hebrew word *re'em* represented a strong animal with something dangerous on its brow. The scholars translated *re'em* to the Greek word *monokeros*. Many people believe that *re'em* may have meant "wild ox" or "buffalo."

Unicorn Tapestry

At one time in Europe, popular stories were woven into tapestries. These were large pieces of cloth depicting figures and images. The Dutch tapestry shown above was created around 1500. It features a unicorn in the upper-left corner. Look closely at the scene displayed. How does this compare with the information you read about beliefs in unicorns during this time?

a part of everyday life in Western culture. By the Middle Ages, the idea of the unicorn was widespread across Europe.

The Holy Hunt

One of the most well-known Western unicorn legends of the Middle Ages was the Holy Hunt. This legend

According to the Holy Hunt, only an innocent young woman can charm a unicorn. Here a unicorn purifies poison water with its horn.

evolved from the unicorn first described in the *Physiologus*. According to the Holy Hunt legend, only a maiden who was pure of heart was able to capture a unicorn. The maiden first went into the forest. When she called the unicorn, it would come to her. Then the unicorn was said to lay its head on her lap and fall asleep. When this happened, hunters would pounce on the unicorn and kill it for its horn.

The Holy Hunt is an example of an allegory. Allegories are stories where the people or animals in the stories really represent something else. The stories often have lessons on how people should behave.

In Christian unicorn legends, the creatures came to represent Jesus.

In Middle Ages Europe, most people practiced the Christian religion. Middle Ages allegories often related to the Christian Bible and its teachings. In the Holy Hunt, the unicorn in the story represents Jesus. According to the Bible, Jesus is the Son of God who is killed but rises from the dead. His death allows God to forgive the sins of others.

The Holy Hunt became a widely popular story during the Middle Ages. Because the unicorn represented Jesus, the animal was shown as pure white and beautiful. This story helped shape the image of the unicorn we know today.

Ctesias described a unicorn-like creature in a book he wrote about India in the 400s BCE:

> There are in India certain wild [donkeys] which are as large as horses and even larger. Their bodies are white, their heads dark red, and their eyes dark blue. They have a horn in the middle of the forehead that is about a foot and a half in length. The dust filed from this horn is administered in a potion as a protection against deadly drugs. The base of this horn, for some two hands'-breadth above the brow, is pure white; the upper part is sharp and of a vivid crimson; and the remainder, or middle portion, is black. Those who drink out of these horns, made into drinking vessels, are not subject, they say, to convulsions or to the holy disease [epilepsy]. Indeed, they are immune even to poisons if, either before or after swallowing such, they drink wine, water, or anything else from these beakers.
>
> Source: Odell Shepard. The Lore of the Unicorn. New York: Barnes and Noble, 1967. Print. 26–27.

Changing Minds

Read Ctesias's description carefully. Create a drawing of the animal he is describing. What real-world animal does your drawing look the most like? Write a few sentences about the animal you think Ctesias's source really saw. Make sure to include facts and details to back up your opinion.

CHAPTER FIVE

UNICORNUCOPIA!

Unicorn sightings are rare today. However, in 2008 a deer with one horn was discovered in Italy. People began calling it a uni-deer. Some people called it a unicorn. But most unicorn sightings are wishful thinking or some other animal like the uni-deer. Today most unicorn sightings are from stickers and toys or in books and movies.

In 2008 people around the world were shocked when a real deer in Italy was discovered with a single horn on its head.

The Last Unicorn

One of the most well-known modern unicorn tales was both a book and a movie. *The Last Unicorn* was initially a book written by Peter Beagle in 1968. In 1982 it became an animated movie. The unicorn in this story is very similar to the white, gentle unicorn of European legends.

In *The Last Unicorn*, a unicorn fears she is the last of her kind. She decides to search for the rest of the unicorns. On her journey, the terrifying Red Bull attacks her. To save her, a magician turns her into a human. They find a castle to stay in. However, a terrible king rules the castle. The now-human unicorn and the magician learn the king has been hiding the

The Last Unicorn film and novel tell the story of a unicorn who goes on a search to find the rest of the unicorns.

unicorns with the help of the Red Bull. After a battle with the Red Bull, the unicorns are released.

More Books

In 1978 author Madeleine L'Engle published *A Swiftly Tilting Planet*. This book features a unicorn named Gaudior. He is a big, powerful unicorn with wings. Gaudior takes the novel's main character,

Charles Wallace, from place to place. He also protects Charles.

Unicorns also play an important role in the popular Harry Potter book series by J. K. Rowling. The books were published between 1997 and 2007. The books were also made into popular films. In Harry Potter's wizarding world, unicorns are magical creatures. Many magic wands are made with unicorn hair. Drinking unicorn blood is said to sustain or prolong life. Harry Potter's unicorns are white, majestic, horse-like creatures. These unicorns are very similar to the creatures of Western legends.

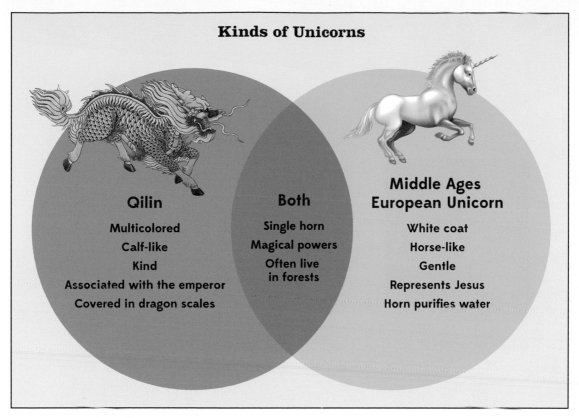

Kinds of Unicorns

Qilin

Multicolored

Calf-like

Kind

Associated with the emperor

Covered in dragon scales

Both

Single horn

Magical powers

Often live
in forests

**Middle Ages
European Unicorn**

White coat

Horse-like

Gentle

Represents Jesus

Horn purifies water

Kinds of Unicorns

This book had information about many different types of unicorns. This diagram shows some of the key differences between Eastern and Western unicorn myths. After reading this book, what characteristics could you add to this diagram? Where would the modern unicorn stories discussed in this chapter fit best?

Unicorns have played an important role in many world cultures for thousands of years. Although few people believe in unicorns today, they are still alive and well in books, movies, and imaginations!

Qilin

China

The story of the qilin was first written down in China thousands of years ago. The qilin looks like a calf with scales like a dragon. It has one horn growing out of its head.

Kirin

Japan

The Japanese kirin has a deer's body and a dragon's head. It also has scales on its body. Some say it has two horns, and some say it has one. According to an ancient legend, the kirin can tell if someone is guilty of a crime.

Karkadann

Persia (modern-day Iran)

The karkadann was the unicorn of ancient Persia. It was a violent creature that looked like a rhinoceros with a black horn and four legs. Each leg had three yellow hooves.

Ctesias's Unicorn

Greece

The first Western written account of the unicorn came from Ctesias in the 400s BCE. Ctesias's unicorn had a white body, a dark red head, and dark blue eyes. Its horn was white at the bottom, black in the middle, and red at the tip. The horn could guard against poison.

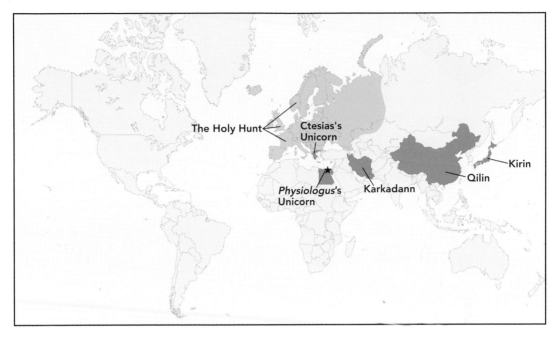

Physiologus's Unicorn
Alexandria, Egypt

The *Physiologus* was written as early as the 100s CE. The unicorn it describes is small and more like a goat than a horse. It is strong, clever, and very hard to catch. The unicorn's magical horn is said to purify poison water.

The Holy Hunt
Europe

The Holy Hunt was a Christian legend from the Middle Ages in which the unicorn represented Jesus. This unicorn was beautiful and pure white. It eventually came to resemble a horse. The Holy Hunt's unicorn was very gentle.

STOP AND THINK

Say What?

The Chinese word for unicorn is *qilin*. Ask an adult to look up how to pronounce the word. How close is it to the word *kirin*? With an adult's help, look online to find out the Chinese character for unicorn. Does it look like a unicorn when you draw it?

Why Do I Care?

Chapter One of this book talks about narwhals. People used to hunt narwhals for their teeth, claiming the teeth were unicorn horns. This was a way to take advantage of a cultural myth for money. Can you think of any ways people today use myths to sell things?

Surprise Me

This book features descriptions of unicorns from both ancient Western and Eastern societies. Some of these unicorns are very different from what we know today. What surprised you most about the descriptions? Why?

You Are There

Imagine you are Ctesias hearing about the unicorn for the first time. What questions would you ask? Write down several interview questions you could ask the travelers to get as much information as you could about this new type of creature.

GLOSSARY

allegory
a story in which people and animals represent something

bellow
a loud animal cry

brutal
cruel or violent

epilepsy
a medical condition that affects the brain, causing someone to black out or lose control over movement

folktale
a story passed down over time

lair
a place where a wild animal sleeps and rests

lore
traditional stories or beliefs

lure
attract

Middle Ages
a period of European history ranging from approximately the 400s to the 1400s CE

philosopher
a person who looks for wisdom and knowledge

phoenix
a mythical bird that dies by starting on fire and then rises from its own ashes

prophecy
a prediction about the future

LEARN MORE

Books

Coville, Bruce, comp. and ed. *The Unicorn Treasury*. Orlando, FL: Magic Carpet Books, 2004.

Hamilton, John. *Unicorns and Other Magical Creatures*. Edina, MN: ABDO, 2005.

Penner, Lucille Recht. *Unicorns*. New York: Random House, 2005.

Web Links

To learn more about unicorns, visit ABDO Publishing Company online at **www.abdopublishing.com**. Web sites about unicorns are featured on our Book Links page. These links are routinely monitored and updated to provide the most current information available.

Visit **www.mycorelibrary.com** for free additional tools for teachers and students.

INDEX

ABOUT THE AUTHOR

Megan Atwood is a writer, teacher, and editor in Minneapolis, Minnesota. She lives with two very real cats and a wonderful human who she has a hard time believing is real at times.